GW00731719

A CINEMATIC GALLERY

• •

80 ORIGINAL IMAGES TO COLOUR AND INSPIRE

ILLUSTRATIONS BY J.M. DRAGUNAS

Titan
BOOKS
London

CHAPTER 1

Harry Potter and the Sorcerer's Stone

In *Harry Potter and the Sorcerer's Stone*, we meet a young boy with a lightning-shaped scar and a tragic history. But everything changes on his eleventh birthday when he makes a shocking discovery: he's a wizard. *Harry Potter and the Sorcerer's Stone* introduces an enchanting world of magic and Muggles, cauldrons and Quidditch, talking portraits and singing hats. And in the center of it all is a boy whose destiny is far greater than anyone imagined.

PROFESSOR McGONAGALL: *"This boy will be famous. There won't be a child in our world who doesn't know his name."*

PROFESSOR DUMBLEDORE: *"Exactly. He's far better off growing up away from all of that, until he's ready."*

—Harry Potter and the Sorcerer's Stone

"They're the worst sort of Muggles imaginable."

—PROFESSOR McGONAGALL, *Harry Potter and the Sorcerer's Stone*

"No post on Sundays, ha! No blasted letters today! No sir!
Not one single bloody letter!"

—UNCLE VERNON, *Harry Potter and the Sorcerer's Stone*

"Welcome, Harry, to Diagon Alley."

—HAGRID, *Harry Potter and the Sorcerer's Stone*

"Right, then. This way to the boats! Come on now, follow me!"

—HAGRID, *Harry Potter and the Sorcerer's Stone*

"When I call your name, you will come forth, I shall place the Sorting Hat on your head, and you will be sorted into your houses."

—PROFESSOR McGONAGALL, *Harry Potter and the Sorcerer's Stone*

"The trick with any beast is to know how to calm him. Take Fluffy, for example. Just play him a bit of music and he falls straight to sleep!"

—HAGRID, *Harry Potter and the Sorcerer's Stone*

"This is no graveyard. It's a chess board."

—RON WEASLEY, *Harry Potter and the Sorcerer's Stone*

CHAPTER 2

Harry Potter and the Chamber of Secrets

At the beginning of *Harry Potter and the Chamber of Secrets*, Dobby
the house-elf warns that terrible things are going to happen at
Hogwarts this year. It doesn't take long for his warnings to come
true. Harry hears strange voices inside the walls, voices seemingly
connected to a series of nasty incidents targeting Muggle-born
students and an old school legend about the mysterious Chamber
of Secrets. With the fate of the school at stake, it's once again
up to Harry to uncover the truth.

"Harry Potter must say he is not going back to school."

—DOBBY, *Harry Potter and the Chamber of Secrets*

RON WEASLEY: *"It's not much, but it's home."*

HARRY POTTER: *"I think it's brilliant."*

—Harry Potter and the Chamber of Secrets

"*Ronald Weasley! How dare you steal that car? I am absolutely disgusted.*"

—MOLLY WEASLEY, *Harry Potter and the Chamber of Secrets*

"I'll ask you three to just nip the rest of them back into their cage."

—PROFESSOR LOCKHART, *Harry Potter and the Chamber of Secrets*

DRACO MALFOY: *"Scared, Potter?"*

HARRY POTTER: *"You wish."*

—Harry Potter and the Chamber of Secrets

"Harry, it was me. But I swear, I didn't mean to. Riddle made me."

—GINNY WEASLEY, *Harry Potter and the Chamber of Secrets*

"Let's match the power of Lord Voldemort, heir of Salazar Slytherin, against the famous Harry Potter."

—TOM RIDDLE, *Harry Potter and the Chamber of Secrets*

CHAPTER 3

Harry Potter and the Prisoner of Azkaban

Harry returns for his third year at Hogwarts, a year that
introduces him to new classes, new teachers, and new magic.
But he also must cope with an unexpected threat: notorious
mass murderer Sirius Black has escaped from prison and,
if rumor is to be believed, he's coming for Harry. *Harry Potter
and the Prisoner of Azkaban* explores some of the key factors
behind the tragedy of Harry's past: his parents' death
and the surprising connection to Black that helps shape
the person Harry becomes.

"Vernon! Vernon, do something!"

—AUNT MARGE, *Harry Potter and the Prisoner of Azkaban*

"Who is that? Who is . . . that is Sirius Black, that is.
  Don't tell me you've never been hearing of Sirius Black?"

—STAN SHUNPIKE, *Harry Potter and the Prisoner of Azkaban*

HAVE YOU SEEN THIS WIZARD?

APPROACH WITH EXTREME CAUTION!

★ DO NOT ATTEMPT TO USE MAGIC AGAINST THIS MAN! ★

Any information leading to the arrest of this man shall be duly rewarded

Notify immediately by owl the Ministry of Magic

"Well done! Well done, Harry, well done! I think he may let you ride him now."

—HAGRID, *Harry Potter and the Prisoner of Azkaban*

"What really finishes a Boggart is laughter. You need to force it to assume a shape you find truly amusing."

"Turn to page three hundred and ninety-four."

—SEVERUS SNAPE, *Harry Potter and the Prisoner of Azkaban*

"I solemnly swear that I am up to no good."

—HARRY POTTER, *Harry Potter and the Prisoner of Azkaban*

"My dear, from the first moment you stepped foot in my class, I sensed that you did not possess the proper spirit for the noble art of Divination . . . You may be young in years, but the heart that beats beneath your bosom is as shriveled as an old maid's, your soul as dry as the pages of the books to which you so desperately cleave."

—PROFESSOR TRELAWNEY, *Harry Potter and the Prisoner of Azkaban*

"Expecto Patronum!"

—HARRY POTTER, *Harry Potter and the Prisoner of Azkaban*

"You know the laws, Miss Granger. You must not be seen, and you would do well, I feel, to return before this last chime. If not, the consequences are too ghastly to discuss."

—PROFESSOR DUMBLEDORE, *Harry Potter and the Prisoner of Azkaban*

CHAPTER 4

Harry Potter and the Goblet of Fire

Harry Potter and the Goblet of Fire sees the Triwizard
Tournament come to Hogwarts, along with students from
two new wizarding schools, several exotic magical creatures,
and a host of exciting new characters. When Harry becomes
the unexpected fourth champion in the tournament, he needs
all his skill—and his friends' help—to survive the tasks and
unravel the mystery of who put his name in the Goblet of Fire.
Meanwhile Dark Forces are gathering in the wizarding world,
bringing Harry closer and closer to an explosive confrontation
that will change everything.

"Now we're all settled in and sorted, I'd like to make an announcement. This castle will not only be your home this year, but home to some very special guests as well."

—PROFESSOR DUMBLEDORE, *Harry Potter and the Goblet of Fire*

"For now please join me in welcoming the lovely ladies of the Beauxbatons Academy of Magic!"

—PROFESSOR DUMBLEDORE, *Harry Potter and the Goblet of Fire*

"Blimey, it's him. Viktor Krum."

—RON WEASLEY, *Harry Potter and the Goblet of Fire*

"The Goblet of Fire—anyone wishing to submit themselves to the tournament need only write their name upon a piece of parchment and throw it in the flame before this hour on Thursday night."

—PROFESSOR DUMBLEDORE, *Harry Potter and the Goblet of Fire*

"Alastor Moody. Ex-Auror, Ministry malcontent, and your new Defense Against the Dark Arts teacher."

—PROFESSOR MOODY, *Harry Potter and the Goblet of Fire*

GEORGE WEASLEY: *"Ready, Fred?"*

FRED WEASLEY: *"Ready, George!"*

BOTH: *"Bottoms up!"*

—Harry Potter and the Goblet of Fire

"Harry Potter?"

—PROFESSOR DUMBLEDORE, *Harry Potter and the Goblet of Fire*

"So tell me, Harry, here you sit a mere boy of twelve, about to compete against three students not only vastly more emotionally mature than yourself, but who have mastered spells that you wouldn't attempt in your dizziest daydreams. Concerned?"

—RITA SKEETER, *Harry Potter and the Goblet of Fire*

"Dragons! That's the first task?"

—HARRY POTTER, *Harry Potter and the Goblet of Fire*

"I look like my Great Aunt Tessie! I smell like my Great Aunt Tessie. Murder me, Harry."

—RON WEASLEY, *Harry Potter and the Goblet of Fire*

RON WEASLEY: *"Poor kid. Bet she's alone in her room crying her eyes out."*

HARRY POTTER: *"Who?"*

RON: *"Hermione, of course. Come on, Harry. Why do you think she wouldn't tell us who she was coming with? Nobody asked her. I would have taken her meself if she wasn't so bloody proud."*

—Harry Potter and the Goblet of Fire

"Earlier today, Professor Moody placed the Triwizard Cup deep within the maze. Only he knows its exact position."

—PROFESSOR DUMBLEDORE, *Harry Potter and the Goblet of Fire*

"The first person to touch the cup will be the winner!"

—PROFESSOR DUMBLEDORE, *Harry Potter and the Goblet of Fire*

CHAPTER 5

Harry Potter and the Order of the Phoenix

Harry struggles to come to terms with the return of Lord Voldemort
in the series' fifth film, *Harry Potter and the Order of the Phoenix.* While
the larger wizarding world turns a blind eye, Harry is introduced to
the Order of the Phoenix, an underground resistance group dedicated
to fighting the Dark Lord. But the real fight wages in Harry's mind,
in the sinister mental link he shares with Voldemort. When a vision
leads him into a devastating trap, Harry finally learns the truth about
his scar and the destiny he cannot escape.

HARRY POTTER: *"Professor Moody, what are you doing here?"*

PROFESSOR MOODY: *"Rescuing you, of course."*

—Harry Potter and the Order of the Phoenix

"You're not going mad. I can see them too. You're just as sane as I am."

—LUNA LOVEGOOD, *Harry Potter and the Order of the Phoenix*

"You're a really good teacher, Harry. I've never been able to stun anything before."

—CHO CHANG, *Harry Potter and the Order of the Phoenix*

"Fourteen years ago, a Death Eater named Bellatrix Lestrange used the Cruciatus Curse on my parents. She tortured them for information, but they never gave in. I'm quite proud to be their son."

—NEVILLE LONGBOTTOM, *Harry Potter and the Order of the Phoenix*

"Kreacher lives to serve the noble House of Black."

—KREACHER, *Harry Potter and the Order of the Phoenix*

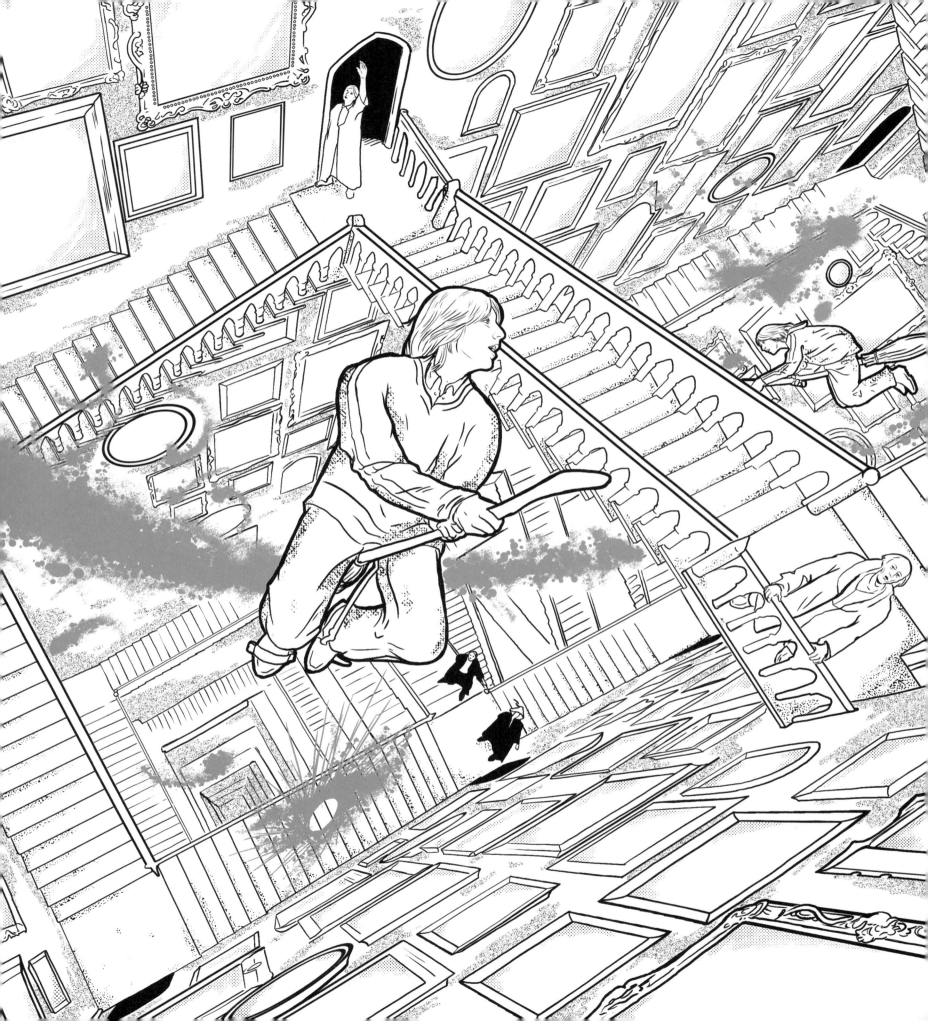

"Ready when you are!"

—FRED WEASLEY, *Harry Potter and the Order of the Phoenix*

"I've waited fourteen years. I guess I can wait a little longer. Now!"

—HARRY POTTER, *Harry Potter and the Order of the Phoenix*

PROFESSOR DUMBLEDORE: *"It was foolish of you to come here tonight, Tom. The Aurors are on their way."*

LORD VOLDEMORT: *"By which time, I shall be gone and you shall be dead."*

—*Harry Potter and the Order of the Phoenix*

CHAPTER 6

Harry Potter and the Half-Blood Prince

Harry's sixth year at Hogwarts turns out to be his last in *Harry Potter and the Half-Blood Prince*. With the Dark Lord getting stronger every day, Professor Dumbledore guides Harry through memories of Voldemort's past, searching for the key to his destruction. Meanwhile Death Eaters target Hogwarts, determined to penetrate its magical protections. And they have a secret weapon: a traitor in the school whose actions will affect Harry's life in ways he never imagined.

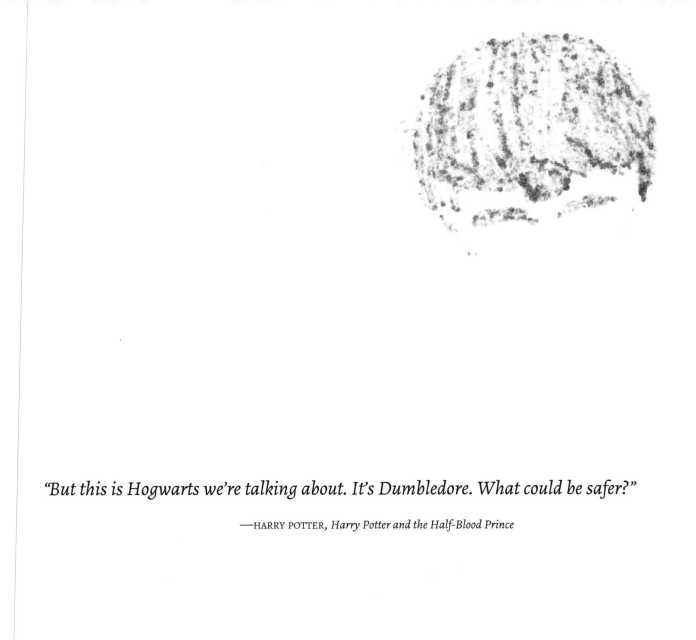

"*But this is Hogwarts we're talking about. It's Dumbledore. What could be safer?*"

—HARRY POTTER, *Harry Potter and the Half-Blood Prince*

RON WEASLEY: *"How much for this?"*

FRED AND GEORGE WEASLEY: *"Five Galleons."*

RON: *"How much for me?"*

FRED AND GEORGE: *"Five Galleons."*

RON: *"I'm your brother."*

FRED AND GEORGE: *"Ten Galleons."*

—Harry Potter and the Half-Blood Prince

HERMIONE GRANGER: *"How did you do that?"*

HARRY POTTER: *"Crush it, don't cut it."*

HERMIONE: *"No. The instructions specifically say to cut."*

—Harry Potter and the Half-Blood Prince

"Here we are then, as promised. One vial of Felix Felicis. Congratulations! Use it well."

—PROFESSOR SLUGHORN, *Harry Potter and the Half-Blood Prince*

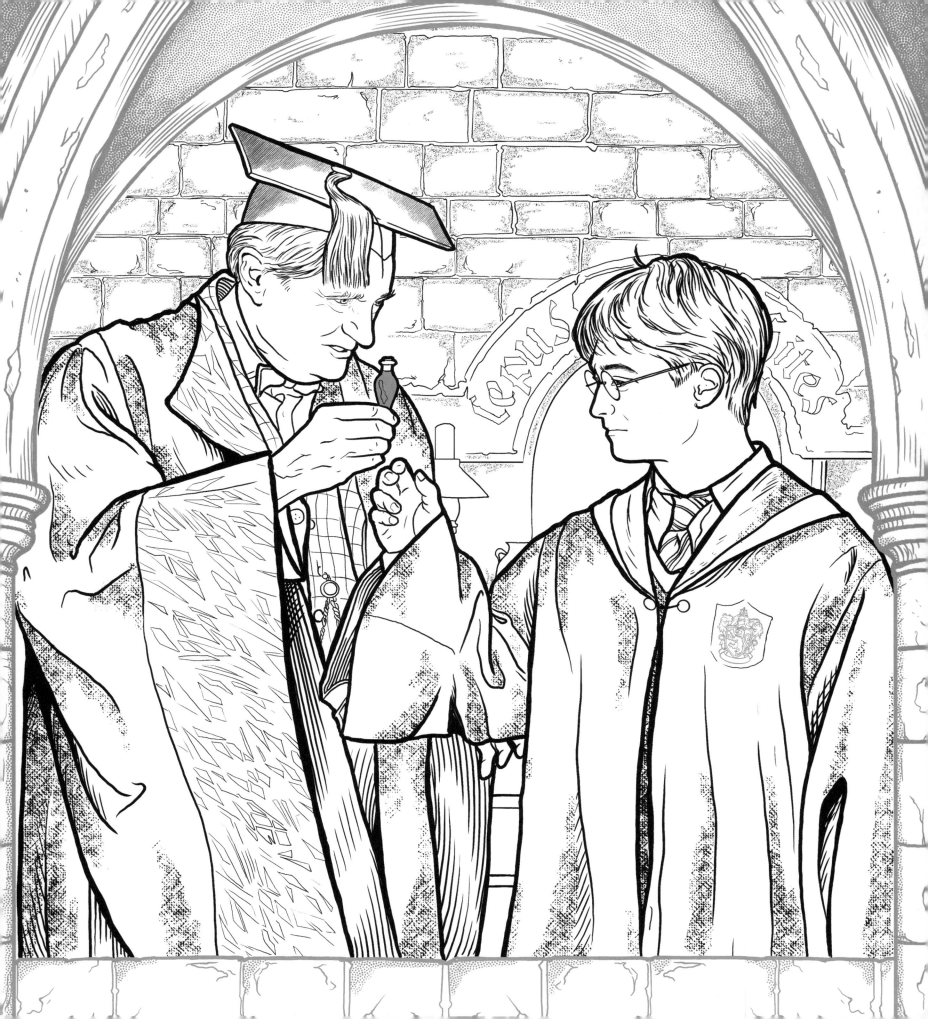

"This vial contains the most particular memory of the day I first met him. I'd like you to see it, if you would."

—PROFESSOR DUMBLEDORE, *Harry Potter and the Half-Blood Prince*

"Hello, everyone. You look dreadful, Ron. Is that why you put something in his cup? Is it a tonic?"

—LUNA LOVEGOOD, *Harry Potter and the Half-Blood Prince*

"That can stay hidden up here too, if you like."

—GINNY WEASLEY, *Harry Potter and the Half-Blood Prince*

"The place to which we journey tonight is extremely dangerous. I promised you could accompany me and I stand by that promise, but there is one condition: you must obey every command I give you without question."

—PROFESSOR DUMBLEDORE, *Harry Potter and the Half-Blood Prince*

"He trusts me. I was chosen."

—DRACO MALFOY, *Harry Potter and the Half-Blood Prince*

"Severus, please."

—PROFESSOR DUMBLEDORE, *Harry Potter and the Half-Blood Prince*

CHAPTER 7

Harry Potter and the Deathly Hallows – Part 1

In the penultimate film of the series, the Dark Lord has overthrown the Ministry of Magic, Hogwarts is under the control of Death Eaters, and the wizarding world is at war. With Ron and Hermione's help, Harry sets off to hunt down and destroy Voldemort's Horcruxes. In doing so, he uncovers a connection to the mythical Deathly Hallows—three magical objects that make the bearer the master of death. Lives are lost, secrets are revealed, and friendships are tested beyond their limits as *Harry Potter and the Deathly Hallows – Part 1* launches the series into its final chapter.

"I believe you're familiar with this particular brew?"

—PROFESSOR MOODY, *Harry Potter and the Deathly Hallows – Part 1*

"There I was, flogging me wares in Diagon Alley, when some Ministry hag comes up and asks to see me license. Says she's a mind to lock me up. Would've done too, if she hadn't taken a fancy to that locket."

—MUNDUNGUS FLETCHER, *Harry Potter and the Deathly Hallows – Part 1*

HARRY POTTER: *"How long did you say this batch of Polyjuice would last, Hermione?"*

HERMIONE GRANGER: *"I didn't."*

—*Harry Potter and the Deathly Hallows – Part 1*

HARRY POTTER: *"Do you think they'd be in there, Hermione? My mum and dad."*

HERMIONE GRANGER: *"Yeah, I think they would."*

—Harry Potter and the Deathly Hallows – Part 1

HARRY POTTER: *"And you cast the doe as well, did you?"*

RON WEASLEY: *"No, I thought that was you."*

—*Harry Potter and the Deathly Hallows – Part 1*

HERMIONE GRANGER: *"What's going on in there?"*

HARRY POTTER AND RON WEASLEY: *". . . Nothing."*

—Harry Potter and the Deathly Hallows – Part 1

"They were angry, you see, about what I'd been writing. So they took her. They took my Luna."

—XENOPHILIUS LOVEGOOD, *Harry Potter and the Deathly Hallows – Part 1*

"Dobby has no master. Dobby is a free elf, and Dobby has come to save Harry Potter and his friends!"

—DOBBY, *Harry Potter and the Deathly Hallows – Part 1*

"The Elder Wand lies with him, of course. Buried in the earth. Dumbledore."

—GELLERT GRINDLEWALD, *Harry Potter and the Deathly Hallows – Part 1*

CHAPTER 8

Harry Potter and the Deathly Hallows – Part 2

The beloved magical saga ends in the ultimate showdown between good and evil, light and dark, love and hate. With the final Horcruxes in sight, Harry, Ron, and Hermione reunite with their fiercest allies to overthrow Lord Voldemort in the climactic Battle of Hogwarts. But it is Harry who must make the ultimate sacrifice to defeat the Dark Lord. *Harry Potter and the Deathly Hallows – Part 2* brings the story to a stunning, emotional conclusion as Harry proves that a true hero will go to any length to save those he loves.

GRIPHOOK: *"You buried the elf?"*

HARRY POTTER: *"Yes."*

GRIPHOOK: *"And brought me here. You are a very unusual wizard."*

—*Harry Potter and the Deathly Hallows – Part 2*

"I've got something, but it's mad."

—HERMIONE GRANGER, *Harry Potter and the Deathly Hallows – Part 2*

RON WEASLEY: *"Don't remember this on the Marauder's Map."*

NEVILLE LONGBOTTOM: *"That's because it never existed until now. The seven secret passages were sealed off before the start of the year. This is the only way in or out now."*

—Harry Potter and the Deathly Hallows – Part 2

"You have something of mine. I'd like it back."

—DRACO MALFOY, *Harry Potter and the Deathly Hallows – Part 2*

PROFESSOR DUMBLEDORE: *"Lily? After all this time?"*

PROFESSOR SNAPE: *"Always."*

—Harry Potter and the Deathly Hallows – Part 2

"People die every day. Friends. Family. Yeah, we lost Harry tonight. But he's still with us, in here. So is Fred and Remus. Tonks. All of them. They didn't die in vain. But you will because you're wrong. Harry's heart did beat for us. For all of us. It's not over."

—NEVILLE LONGBOTTOM, *Harry Potter and the Deathly Hallows – Part 2*

"Come on, Tom. Let's finish this the way we started it. Together."

—HARRY POTTER, *Harry Potter and the Deathly Hallows – Part 2*

TITAN
BOOKS

A division of Titan Publishing Group Ltd
144 Southwark Street
London SE1 0UP

www.titanbooks.com

 Find us on Facebook: www.facebook.com/TitanBooks
 Follow us on Twitter: @titanbooks

Published by Titan Books, London, in 2017.

Published by arrangement with Insight Editions, PO Box 3088, San Rafael, CA 94912, USA.
www.insighteditions.com

A CIP catalogue record for this title is available from the British Library.
ISBN: 9781785657405

Publisher: Raoul Goff
Associate Publisher: Vanessa Lopez
Art Director: Chrissy Kwasnik
Designers: Leah Bloise, Ashley Quackenbush
Sponsoring Editor: Greg Solano
Managing Editor: Alan Kaplan
Editorial Assistant: Hilary VandenBroek
Production Editor: Rachel Anderson
Production Manager: Alix Nicholaeff and Lina s Palma
Production Assistant: Pauline Kerkhove Sellin

All illustrations by J.M. Dragunas, with retouching by Robin F. Williams
Black Family tapestry illustration by Frans Boukas

Insight Editions, in association with Roots of Peace, will plant two trees for each tree used in the manufacturing of this book. Roots of Peace is an internationally renowned humanitarian organization dedicated to eradicating land mines worldwide and converting war-torn lands into productive farms and wildlife habitats. Roots of Peace will plant two million fruit and nut trees in Afghanistan and provide farmers there with the skills and support necessary for sustainable land use.

Manufactured in China

10 9 8 7 6 5 4 3 2 1